Papa and I Have Purple Feet!

By Phil Notarange

Illustrations by Alison Z. Pitts

It was harvest time at the vineyard nearby

So Papa and I thought we would give it a try.

I grabbed my blue pail and put on my old shirt

And ran down to the vineyard through grass and

through dirt.

When we got to the vines with the grapes hanging low

Papa looked at me and said, "Are you ready? Let's go!"

We were careful with the snips so I wouldn't get hurt

But also with the grapes to not fall in the dirt.

4

Although the first grapes we cut were a nice color and round

We thought there were better ones, so we looked all around.

We walked up and down rows of vines full of fruit

I wanted to fill my pail with all of this loot!

The vines were everywhere and the vineyard was full

Of so many grapes, Papa said, "Hey Nate, this is cool!"

My hands too small to carry all the fruit of the vine

So I placed them gently in this blue pail of mine.

This was so much fun for my Papa and me
I didn't want to stop picking each little berry.
And when I did find the perfect bunch, "Oh my!"
I grabbed it and held it up high in the sky!

We searched and we harvested all day in the sun

I like when Papa makes wine but this is more fun!

I was already thinking of what I would say

When I got home to tell Mom about my great day.

Of the grapes in my pail there were only a few

I wanted to fill it but didn't know what to do.

Then Papa said, "Don't worry Nate, I know how

Cause I will help you with picking the grapes right now."

14

We searched and we picked the best grapes we could find

It took many hours but we did not mind.

I reached for some grapes that were up kind of high

I stooped down for others that were low and nearby.

I was getting a bit tired, the grapes we had enough

The pail was heavy now but carrying it wasn't tough.

I like playing outside in the warmth of the sun

But picking grapes at harvest is so much more fun!

The harvest was finished, I wanted to rest

And like everything else I gave it my best.

Carrying the pail of grapes I wanted to run

Little did I know our work had just begun.

Just picking the grapes is only part of the task

To make the best wine "There is more?" I asked.

Papa said "Just the berries, not stems, Grandson."

From the pile on the table, I knew I wasn't done.

22

Papa said to remove each grape from the stem

I could do it myself with no help from him.

I was focused; I knew I could do it all right

Using all of my strength and all of my might.

24

With the grapes in the bucket it was time for the test

Could I crush them with my feet without taking a rest?

So I stomped and I stomped but had some time free

For a nice photo of Papa, Louie, and me!

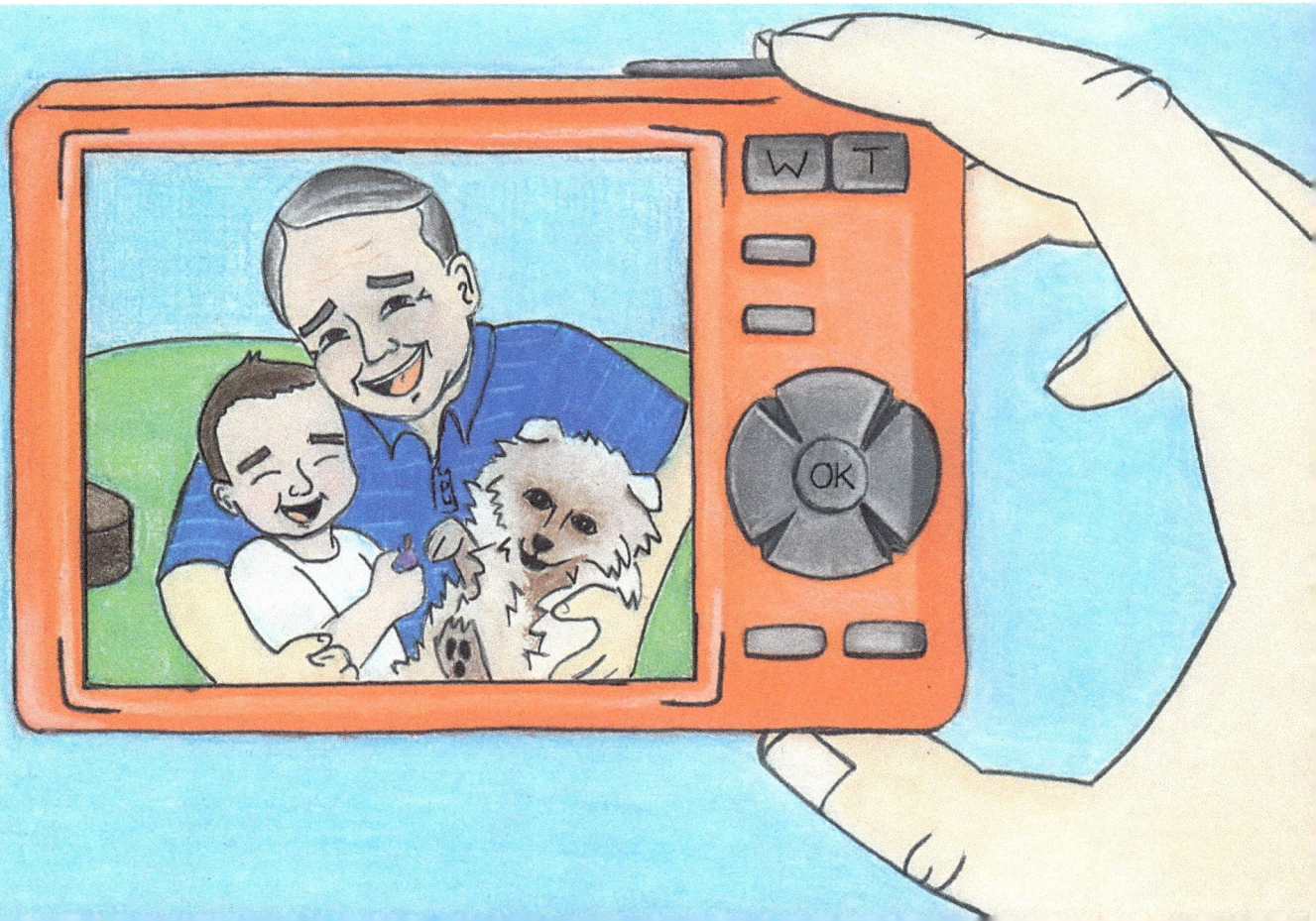

Stomping the grapes was now complete,

When I looked down I said "Wow, I have purple feet!"

With bits of the grapes covering my feet and my toes

I thought "Hey, this is the harvest! That's how it goes!"

28

Now Papa wanted to stomp the grapes too

But only his one foot would fit in my pail of blue.

So we stomped them together, the grapes we did squish

Wow, we finally did it! This was our wish!

Our day at the vineyard at last was complete

Because Papa and I now have purple feet!

It was fun on this special day just like we knew

We love having purple feet. Would you like them too?

www.ingramcontent.com/pod-product-compliance
Lightning Source LLC
Chambersburg PA
CBHW040304100426
42811CB00011B/1352